Bond Assessment Papers

Fourth papers in English

J M Bond and Sarah Lindsay

Key words

Some special words are used in this book. You will find them picked out in **bold** in the Papers. These words are explained here.

abbreviation	a word or words which are shortened
adjective	a word that describes somebody or something
adverb	a word that gives extra meaning to a verb
alphabetical order	words arranged in the order found in the alphabet
antonym	a word with a meaning opposite to another word *hot – cold*
clause	a section of a sentence with a verb
main clause	a clause in a sentence which makes sense on its own
subordinate clause	gives more information about and is dependent on the main clause
compound word	a word made up of two other words *football*
conditional	a clause or sentence expressing the idea that one thing depends on something else
conjunction	a word used to link sentences, phrases or words *and, but*
connective	a word or words that join clauses or sentences
contraction	two words shortened into one with an apostrophe placed where the letter/s have been dropped *do not = don't*
definition	meanings of words
diminutive	a word implying smallness *booklet*
homophone	words that have the same sound as another but a different meaning or spelling *right / write*
metaphor	a figurative expression in which something is described in terms usually associated with another *the sky is a <u>sapphire sea</u>*
noun	a word for somebody or something
collective noun	a word referring to a group *swarm*
proper noun	the names of people, places, etc. *Ben*
abstract noun	a word referring to a concept or idea *love*
object	a noun referring to a person or thing which is affected by the action of a verb *He ate an <u>ice-cream</u>*
onomatopoeic	a word that echoes a sound, associated with its meaning *hiss*
past tense	something that has already happened
phrase	a group of words that act as a unit
adjectival phrase	a group of words describing a noun
plural	more than one *cats*
prefix	a group of letters added to the beginning of a word *un, dis*
preposition	a word that relates other words to each other *he sat <u>behind</u> me, the book <u>on</u> the table*
pronoun	words often replacing nouns
reported speech	what has been said without using the exact words or speech marks
root word	words to which prefixes or suffixes can be added to make other words *<u>quick</u>ly*
sentence	a unit of written language which makes sense by itself
complex sentence	a sentence containing a main clause and subordinate clause(s)
simile	an expression to describe what something is like *as cold as ice*
singular	one *cat*
subject	the person or thing who does the action expressed by the verb *<u>the lion</u> roared*
suffix	a group of letters added to the end of a word *ly, ful*
superlative	describes the limit of a quality (adjective or adverb) *most/least* or *shortest*
synonym	words with a very similar meaning to another word *quick – fast*
verb	a 'doing' or 'being' word
active	when the main person or thing does the action *he <u>took</u> it*
passive	when the main person or thing has the action done to it *it <u>was taken</u> by him*

Paper 1

"Inspector, please tell me about beachcombers – your voluntary helpers. Are more needed, and how do they set about being taken on?"

With a friendly grin he replied, "Of course more are needed. In the first three months of this year our counters, or beachcombers, reported 20,000 dead birds, a large number of which were the victims of pollution in Britain, and make no mistake, it can happen again. So, yes, we want more helpers. All young people interested in this work should contact their local RSPCA inspectors as soon as they hear of an oil disaster. That is the emergency help we need. As to regular voluntary work, contact the Royal Society for the Protection of Birds and ask to help with their beached bird survey around the coast of Britain."

Underline the right answers.

1 A volunteer is (a bird watcher, a soldier, a person who works without being paid).

2 The counters are (people who count birds, rings on birds, a kind of bird, a kind of shell).

3 Beachcombers are (people who live on the beach, people who search for things on the beach, campers).

Answer these questions.

4 In January, February and March how many dead birds were found?

_____

5 Write what you think 'make no mistake' means.

_____

6 What do you think RSPCA stands for?

_____

7–8 What are the two ways in which you could help?

_____

_____

9 What do you think causes the oil pollution that kills so many sea birds?

_____

Write the **plural** form of these words.

10	butterfly	_____	**11**	melody	_____
12	cup	_____	**13**	echo	_____
14	knife	_____	**15**	banana	_____
16	puppy	_____	**17**	sweet	_____

Rewrite each of the following, using only two words, one of which should have an apostrophe.

e.g. basket for a cat   _cat's basket_

18 school for girls   _____

19 hospital for women   _____

20 canteen for the workers   _____

21 playground for children   _____

22 ward reserved for men   _____

23 ball for a dog   _____

24 wheel of a car   _____

Put these words in **alphabetical order**.

25–30 procure   (1) _____

product   (2) _____

probe   (3) _____

produce   (4) _____

process   (5) _____

proceed   (6) _____

In each sentence underline the **object** and write a **pronoun** for each **subject**.

31–32   Bill hit the ball.   subject pronoun _____

33–34   The young girl cut her knee.   subject pronoun _____

35–36   The children in the school sang a song.   subject pronoun _____

37–38   The football team won the cup.   subject pronoun _____   **8**

Rewrite these statements as questions, changing as few words as possible.

   e.g. Paper boys work on Saturdays.
        Do paper boys work on Saturdays?

39   The weather is cold outside.

   _____

40   Bill and Emma are going on holiday.

   _____

41   We should leave our boots outside.

   _____

42   My head aches.

   _____

43   The dog enjoyed his walk on the moor.

   _____

44   We never use the old grandfather clock.

   _____   **6**

Write the word with a *ure* **suffix** that is related to each of these words.

45   press   _____   46   enclose   _____

47   fail   _____   48   depart   _____

49   please   _____   50   furnish   _____

51   expose   _____   52   moist   _____   **8**

Write a **synonym** for the words in bold.

53 The twins were **exactly the same** in all ways.   _____

54 The concert was **put off** until next week.   _____

55 She **made up her mind** to make a cake.   _____

56 The army **went forward** to attack.   _____

57 They had a party **once a year**.   _____

58 As most of the team were ill, the match was **called off**.   _____

59 The bread is **not fresh**.   _____

Circle the *unstressed syllable* in each of these words.

60 t r a v e l   61 d e s p a i r   62 c o m p l a i n t

63 r e p e l   64 b u t t o n   65 p o s t a g e

66 m o l t e n   67 s i l v e r   68 m e t a l

Rewrite these sentences without double negatives.

69 Damien didn't want no food.

_____

70 There weren't no footballs in the shed.

_____

71 There wasn't no water in the paddling pool.

_____

72 Nina hadn't no problem with ice-skating.

_____

73 Jane didn't buy no sweets from the shop.

_____

Finish these similes, using your own words.

74 as white as   _____

75 as busy as a   _____

76 as thick as   _____

77   as pretty as a _____

78   as quick as a _____

79   as hot as _____

6

Rewrite the passage correctly, starting a new line when a different person starts to speak.

80–95   Where are we going asked a shivering Ben To the haunted house replied
Danielle I haven't got my boots on and we have to cross the stream exclaimed
Ben Never mind Danielle laughed

_____

_____

_____

_____

_____

_____

_____

16

Add a **conjunction** to each of these sentences.

96   The children kept very quiet _____ their teacher walked past them.

97   Verity went home after dinner _____ she wasn't feeling well.

98   The dogs waited for their walk _____ the children put their coats on.

99   On Christmas Eve Daniel couldn't fall asleep _____ he was too excited.

100   Kate waited at the gate _____ her mother arrived.

5

100
TOTAL

Paper 2

It did not happen until the fourth day of the summer holidays, and then only by a mere fluke, for if the bright new golden penny had come down tails up they would have helped father to fish instead of exploring by themselves.

"Tails, fish; heads, explore," Keith had said as he tossed for it . . . and it was heads.

At first there were complaints from the other four, for it was great fun helping father to fish; for the children, that is. Father was not overkeen on the assistance of his offspring; but Keith put an instant stop to these iniquitous murmurings.

"Shut up!" he said. "It's disrespectful to the gods not to abide by the toss."

"Why?" demanded Elspeth.

"Because you have challenged them. You have said, 'Speak, oh ye gods! If it is your will that we should help Father fish then show us the flicker of a sparkling tail upon the dust, but if it is your will that we should seek adventure on the high road then show us the outline of a king's head set in gold!'"

"Pick up our penny anyhow," said Elspeth. "It is our only one . . . You pick it up, Flora-Dora."

The fat little twins slid solidly off the wall, picked up the penny, returned it to Elspeth, and climbed heavily back to their seats.

From *A Crock of Gold* by Elizabeth Goudge

Underline the right answers.

1 What is 'a fluke'?
   (a toss, a lucky chance, a golden penny)

2 What did most of the children want to do?
   (go fishing, go exploring, they didn't know)

3 How did the coin land?
   (don't know, heads up, tails up)

3

Answer these questions.

4 How many children were there?

_____

5 Did Father want the children's help?

_____

6 Who was the leader of the children?

_____

7 What are 'offspring'?

_____

8 Why do you think Keith said, "It's disrespectful to the gods not to abide by the toss"?

_____

9 What do you think 'iniquitous' means?

_____

10 What do you think happened on the fourth day of the summer holidays?

_____

7

Write two **adjectives** to describe each of these **nouns**.

11–12 _____ , _____ dog

13–14 _____ , _____ chair

15–16 _____ , _____ castle

17–18 _____ , _____ shop

19–20 _____ , _____ shoes

10

Add the missing commas to these sentences.

21–23 On our holiday we visited many towns, including Bath Bristol Swansea Stafford and York.

24–26 My mum loves listening to her records of Cliff Richard Elvis Presley The Beatles Tina Turner and Michael Jackson.

27–30 My friends are Joe who plays great jokes Raju and Zoe who is my best friend.

10

Underline the **root words** in each of these.

31 pressure   32 subdivide   33 transatlantic

34 disagreement   35 endangered   36 magical

37 frightening   38 trainer

With a line match the beginning of the proverb with its end.

39 A stitch in time   deserves another.

40 Let sleeping dogs   saves nine.

41 Two heads are better   spoil the broth.

42 Practice   than one.

43 Too many cooks   lie.

44 One good turn   makes perfect.

Complete the second **clause** (that includes a verb) for each of these sentences.

45 I saw a burglary taking place while _____

46 Our dog always chases squirrels but _____

47 I went for a run after _____

48 I love swimming in the sea because _____

49 My Nan made me a cake and _____

50 We played in the garden until _____

Circle the masculine words.

51–56   cow   cockerel   prince   waiter

        Mister   husband   queen   nephew

            actress   women

Write *there*, *their* or *they're* in each gap. Don't forget capital letters, if necessary.

57–58 They must get _____ coats from over _____.

59–61 _____ goes _____ cat which _____ giving
       away.

62 Where is _____ breakfast?

10

63–64 _____ always going to have queues if they don't open

all_____ tills.

8

Write **active** or **passive** next to each **sentence**.

65   The dog caught the ball.   _____

66   The cat was injured in a fight.   _____

67   The zoo keeper was bitten by the lion.   _____

68   David climbed the tree.   _____

69   The teacher called the children.   _____

70   Jane was hit by a snowball.   _____

71   The man was taken in the ambulance.   _____

72   Two cows pushed the gate open.   _____

8

Write an **antonym** for each of these words.

73   expand   _____   74   inferior   _____

75   guilty   _____   76   mad   _____

77   question   _____   78   divide   _____

79   reveal   _____   80   elevate   _____

8

Rewrite these sentences, adding the missing punctuation and capital letters.

81–86   the wind strong and gusty blew ninas hat off

_____

87–92   the film is about to start yelled anton

_____

12

Complete these word sums. Don't forget any spelling changes.

93   take + ing   _____   94   lame + ly   _____

95   waste + ful   _____   96   slope + ing _____

97   value + able _____   98   wise + ly   _____

99   shame + ful   _____   100 believe + able _____

8

100
TOTAL

The World below the Brine

The world below the brine,
Forests at the bottom of the sea, the branches
    and leaves,
Sea lettuce, vast lichens, strange flowers and seeds,
    the thick tangle, openings, and pink turf,
Different colours, pale grey and green, purple, white,
    and gold, the play of light through the water,
Dumb swimmers there among the rocks, coral,
    gluten, grass, rushes, and the aliment of swimmers,
Sluggish existences grazing there suspended, or
    slowly crawling close to the bottom,
The sperm whale at the surface blowing air and
    spray, or disporting with his flukes,
The leaden-eyed shark, the walrus, the turtle, the
    hairy sea-leopard, and the sting-ray,
Passions there, wars, pursuits, tribes, sight in those
    ocean-depths, breathing that thick-breathing air,
    as so many do,
The change thence to the sight here, and to the subtle
    air breathed by beings like us who walk this sphere,
The change onward from ours to that of beings who
    walk other spheres.

by Walt Whitman

Underline the right answers.

1 The poem is about (the world beyond the brink, the world below the sea,
tropical forests, outer space).

2 'Brine' is (a bridge, fresh water, a kind of fish, salt water).

3 Which animal is 'hairy'?
(the walrus, the shark, the sea-leopard, the turtle)

Answer these questions.

4–5 Which two words describe creatures which hang motionless or move slowly?

_____ _____

6 At which level in the sea does the sperm whale play?

_____

7 Describe in your own words the eyes of a shark.

_____

8 Why is the water described as 'thick-breathing air'?

_____

9 After reading the poem, do you think 'The world below the brine' is a place where you would like to be able to live? Why?

_____

_____

6

From the **verbs** listed write a **noun** ending in *ion*.

10 divide _____ **11** produce _____

12 dictate _____ **13** create _____

14 invade _____ **15** resolve _____

16 explode _____ **17** lubricate _____

8

Add a **clause** to each of these to make a longer sentence. Use a different **connective** each time.

18–19 Tom slipped, breaking his arm _____

_____

20–21 Tom slipped, breaking his arm _____

_____

22–23 Tom slipped, breaking his arm _____

_____

In each space write the most suitable **adverb**.

longingly   heroically   patiently   attentively

feverishly   thoroughly   spitefully

24 The whole class listened _____ to their teacher.

25 A good worker does a job_____ .

26 To repeat malicious gossip is to talk _____ .

27 The children looked _____ at the presents under the tree.

28 After the crash the rescuers worked _____ .

29 The invalid waited _____ for the doctor to visit her.

30 The men who were trapped dug _____ through the rubble.

Match a word in each column to make a **compound word**.

green   look

day   knife

cloud   light

water   house

pen   knob

door   burst

out   tight

31 _____   **32** _____

33 _____   **34** _____

35 _____   **36** _____

37 _____

Copy this sentence, adding the missing punctuation and capital letters.

38–51   i think ive lost my purse cried mrs davis id better tell the police

_____

_____

_____   `14`

Add *ie* or *ei* to each of these to make a word.

52 c_____ling	**53** l_____sure	**54** _____ght	
55 f_____ld	**56** bel_____ve	**57** rec_____ve	
58 sh_____ld	**59** s_____ze	**60** ach_____ve	

`9`

Write the two words each **contraction** stands for.

61 I'm   _____   _____

62 don't   _____   _____

63 could've   _____   _____

64 you're   _____   _____

65 it's   _____   _____

66 they're   _____   _____

67 let's   _____   _____

`7`

Write a **definition** for each of these words.

68 viewpoint   _____

69 argument   _____

70 conclusion   _____

71 opinion   _____

`4`

Write an interesting sentence, including an **adjective** and an **adverb** in each, using the noun and verb provided.

72–73 cat leapt

_____

74–75 submarine sank

_____

76–77 vase smashed

_____

78–79 magazine opened

_____

Write two **onomatopoeic** words that can describe these.

80–81 fairground _____ _____

82–83 seaside _____ _____

84–85 zoo _____ _____

86–87 playground _____ _____

Add a **prefix** to each of these to make a new word.

88 _____ability **89** _____sure **90** _____plane

91 _____justice **92** _____marine **93** _____direct

94 _____pleasure

Write two comparing **phrases** using each of these words.

e.g. reliable _less reliable/least reliable_

more reliable/most reliable

95–96 cautious

_____

_____

97–98 dependable

_____

_____

99–100 sensible

_____

_____

Paper 4

Luckily for Alice, the little magic bottle had now had its full effect, and she grew no larger: still it was very uncomfortable, and, as there seemed to be no sort of chance of her ever getting out of the room again, no wonder she felt unhappy.

"It was much pleasanter at home," thought poor Alice, "when one wasn't always growing larger and smaller, and being ordered about by mice and rabbits. I almost wish I hadn't gone down that rabbit-hole – and yet – and yet – it's rather curious, you know, this sort of life! I do wonder what *can* have happened to me! When I used to read fairy-tales, I fancied that kind of thing never happened, and now here I am in the middle of one! There ought to be a book written about me, that there ought! And when I grow up, I'll write one – but I'm grown up now," she added in a sorrowful tone; "at least there's no room to grow up any more *here*."

"But then," thought Alice, "shall I *never* get any older than I am now? That'll be a comfort, one way – *never* to be an old woman – but then – always to have lessons to learn! Oh, I shouldn't like *that*!"

"Oh, you foolish Alice!" she answered herself. "How can you learn lessons in here? Why, there's hardly any room for *you*, and no room for any lesson-books!"

And so she went on, taking first one side and then the other, and making quite a conversation of it altogether; but after a few minutes she heard a voice outside, and stopped to listen.

From *Alice's Adventures in Wonderland* by Lewis Carroll

Underline the right answers.

1   How did Alice feel about growing larger?
    (happy, excited, cross, unhappy)

2–3 Who had been ordering Alice about?
    (her mother, rabbits, fairies, mice, an old woman)

4 Who was Alice having a conversation with? [box: 4]
(herself, a rabbit, can't tell)

Answer these questions.

5–6 Why was life more pleasant at home for Alice?

_____

_____

7 Who does Alice think ought to write a book about her?

_____

8 Write why Alice thinks it is good that she might never get older.

_____

9 Why do you think Alice might always have lessons to learn?

_____

10 Why was there no room for any lesson-books?

_____ [box: 6]

Write the following **nouns** in their **plural** form.

11	kangaroo	_____	**12**	atlas	_____
13	deer	_____	**14**	knife	_____
15	mosquito	_____	**16**	louse	_____
17	ox	_____	**18**	chief	_____

[box: 8]

Change the following sentences into **reported speech**.

19 Tom said, "I'll do my homework after I've watched television."

_____

20 "I shall have to change my plans," Mum said.

_____

21 Dad said, "I'm playing cricket this evening."

_____

22 "I forgot to buy Sheena a birthday card," Amanda exclaimed.

_____

23 "Would you like to play football, Tim?" Tony asked.

_____

24 "I'm afraid," Nan said, "it is time to go home."

_____

In which tense is each of these sentences written?

25 He is running to school. _____

26 They will meet at the clubhouse. _____

27 Andy fell out of the tree. _____

28 Sue swam this morning. _____

29 Cats often catch mice. _____

30 They are eating their breakfast. _____

31 Trisha laughed at the clown. _____

Use each word in a sentence to show its meaning. You can add **suffixes** to them.

32 fatigue _____

33 official _____

34 precarious _____

35 renovate _____

36 pedestrian _____

37 submerge _____

Choose the correct **verb** form for each of these sentences.

38 Damien (wash/washes) his football boots each week.

39 My dog (is/are) my best friend.

40 Kate (was/were) very happy on holiday.

41 They (is/are) unsure whether to go to Pete's house.

42 Dad (turn/turns) the tap on.

43 Meena and Tuhil (was/were) very excited about Diwali.

44 The goat (eat/ate) its food. ˏ

45 Hannah (drink/drank) the bottle of ice-cold water.

`8`

Complete each sentence as a **metaphor**.

46 The sea is a raging _____ .

47 The snow is a soft, white _____ .

48 The sun was a golden _____ .

49 The clouds are soft, fluffy _____ .

50 The wind is a howling _____ .

51 The stars were glittering _____ in the sky.

`6`

Rewrite the misspelt words correctly.

52 transparant   _____

53 seperate   _____

54 sucess   _____

55 goverment   _____

56 diffrent   _____

57 vegtables   _____

58 theives   _____

59 dependible   _____

60 libaray   _____

`9`

Form **adjectives** from the words in bold.

61 **sense**   She gave a _____ reply.

62 **Greece**   The _____ olives tasted good.

63 **study**   He is a _____ boy.

64 **energy**   It was an _____ dance.

65 **angel**   She had an _____ voice.

66 **Switzerland**   _____ clocks are very reliable.

67 **triangle**   It was a _____ piece.

`7`

Punctuate these sentences correctly.

68–74 peter called im ready

_____

75–82 when will we get to davids house jake asked

_____

83–92 quick yelled sam we will miss our train

_____

Write two meanings for each of these words. One might be a meaning that has evolved over recent years.

93–94 **cool**

(1) _____

(2) _____

95–96 **trainer**

(1) _____

(2) _____

Add a **suffix** to each word.

ure   ish   ful   able

97 fool   _____

98 grace   _____

99 enclose   _____

100 value   _____

Paper 5

"A man's first mistake in the Arctic is usually his last," says Squadron Leader Scott Alexander of the Royal Canadian Air Force's survival training school at Cambridge Bay, 200 miles inside the Arctic Circle. Here, in a land of snow, ice and rock, mauled by vicious polar winds, a handful of experts are teaching Canadian airmen how to stay alive in the event of an emergency landing.

More than 2,000 students take this course annually. "If you survive, you've passed," the men jest.

The course begins in heavily timbered country in Alberta. Here the thirty or forty men in a group receive ten days instruction in bush experience. Nothing is overlooked that might help a man live through an emergency. Then comes the most gruelling session. Dressed in heavy survival gear and parachute harness, the men fly to Cambridge Bay. Once they have built their snow houses, lit the Primus stoves, and prepared a meal from emergency rations, the outlook brightens. Bedtime comes early because dampness increases the danger of freezing. Socks, mitts, flying boots and shirt all go to bed with the man – to be dried during the night by body heat.

Underline the right answers.

1   A man's first mistake is usually his last because (he learns quickly, a mistake usually causes death, he is only allowed to make one mistake).

2   'Inside the Arctic Circle' means (within the Arctic Circle, trapped in the ice of the Arctic Circle, south of the Arctic Circle).

3   (Thirty, Two hundred, Two thousand) students do the course each year.

| | 3 |

Answer these questions.

4   Which country do the airmen come from?

_____

5   What is the course teaching the airmen to do?

_____

6   How do the airmen dry their clothes?

_____

7   What do you think 'mauled by winds' means?

_____

8   The airmen are on a very tough course. Apart from the first sentence what other information tells you this?

_____

9   What does 'the outlook brightens' mean?

_____

10   If you were on this course which part would you find the hardest?

_____

| | 7 |

Each of these words has an unstressed vowel missing. Rewrite the words correctly.

11   machinry   _____   12   favourte   _____

13   memry   _____   14   sentnce   _____

15   jewellry   _____   16   impatent   _____

17   misrable   _____   18   busness   _____

| | 8 |

Rewrite these sentences changing them from **singular** to **plural**.

19–22   The girl was riding her horse.

_____

23

23–25 The rabbit fled down its burrow.

_____

26–29 He saved the stamp to add to his collection.

_____

Write the words in full of the following **abbreviations**.

30 DIY _____

31 p & p _____

32 c/o _____

33 p.a. _____

34 Bros. _____

35 Ind. Est. _____

36 Dr _____

Write the **nouns** in the correct columns of the table.

37–44   happiness   grass   opinion   team

gang   Harry   flame   December

common nouns	collective nouns	proper nouns	abstract nouns

Write one word instead of the words in bold.

45 We **kept out of the way of** Mum because she was cross. _____

46 Mr Martin says that my work is **getting much better**. _____

47 In case we forgot, we said the message **over and over again**. _____

48 The fraction had to be **turned upside down**. _____

49 **A short time ago** we went to the circus. _____

50 The boy was told to **come back** tomorrow. _____

51 The cyclist knocked over a **person who was walking**. _____

Rewrite the following passage, adding the missing capital letters.

52–61 as zoe and rupa slept soundly strange things began to happen. a night to remember, the book rupa had been reading, suddenly fell open at a page. the page told the story of a ghost which haunted the streets of skegness every thursday night.

_____

_____

_____

_____

_____

10

Add two more words that are based on the following **root words**.

　　　e.g. help　　*helping*　　　　　*helpful*

62–63　love　　_____　　_____

64–65　clear　　_____　　_____

66–67　cycle　　_____　　_____

68–69　pay　　_____　　_____

8

Each of these groups of muddled letters is the name of a country. Which countries are they?

70　rFnaec　　_____　　　**71**　iCahn　　_____

72　kanistaP　　_____　　　**73**　deeSnw　　_____

74　salAturai　　_____　　　**75**　asWel　　_____

76　amicaJa　　_____

7

Underline separately the **clauses** in each sentence.

77–78　Wes thought that he must have been dreaming.

79–80　My Dad collapsed into his chair because the run had exhausted him!

81–82　The picture fell from the wall, glass smashing everywhere.

83–84　Judy wondered whether the book might be useful for her project.

8

These **phrases** are often used in formal letters or documents. What do they mean?

85 further to your recent correspondence

_____

86 forms may be obtained from

_____

87 those wishing to attend

_____

88 notice is hereby served

_____

4

Draw a line (/) every time a new line should have been started in the following dialogue.

89–94 "Where is Jess?" moaned Dad. "We really need to get going or we will miss our ferry." "She is coming. I can hear her racing down the stairs," replied Mum. "About time too!" continued Dad. As Jess climbed into the car, Mum enquired, "Have you got your coat?" "Oops . . . shall I go and get it?" Jess asked. "Yes, and be VERY quick," Dad almost shouted. "I'm losing my patience!" "Sorry," she called as she flew into the house.

6

Write the number of where you think each word has been derived from:

(1) another language

(2) names of places or people

(3) imitating sounds

95 sizzle _____   **96** wellington _____

97 spaghetti _____   **98** splutter _____

99 photograph _____   **100** hoover _____

6

100 TOTAL

Paper 6

Anne Frank was a German Jew living in Holland during the Second World War. At this time Jews were rounded up and sent to concentration camps where many died. Anne Frank and her family went into hiding with another family, the Van Daans, where they lived for over two years before being discovered. While hiding from the Nazis Anne wrote a diary.

Monday, 26th July, 1943

It was about two o'clock . . . when the sirens began to wail . . . We had not been upstairs five minutes when they began shooting hard, so much so that we went and stood in the passage. And yes, the house rumbled and shook, and down came the bombs.

I clasped my 'escape bag' close to me, more because I wanted to have something to hold than with an idea of escaping, because there's nowhere we can go. If ever we come to the extremity of fleeing from here, the street would be just as dangerous as an air raid. This one subsided after half an hour . . .

That evening at dinner: another air raid! It was a nice meal, but at the sound of the alert my hunger vanished . . . 'Oh, dear me, twice in one day, that's too much,' we all thought, but that didn't help at all; once again the bombs rained down . . .

From The Diary of Anne Frank

Underline the right answers.

1 Where were Anne and her family living during the Second World War?
(Germany, Holland, France)

2 How long was Anne in hiding before she was discovered?
(2 months, 2 years, more than 2 years)

3 How long did the air raid at 2 o'clock last?
(five minutes, half an hour, many hours)

Answer these questions.

4 Who else was hiding with Anne and her family?

_____

5 Why did Anne clasp her escape bag?

_____

6 What do you think 'extremity' in this context means?

_____

7 Find a word in the passage meaning 'finished'.

_____

8 Why do you think Anne's hunger vanished at dinner?

_____

9 What do you think Anne might have had in her 'escape bag'?

_____

Write in each gap *to*, *too*, or *two*.

10–12 For Philip's dare he is going _____ climb on the wall, take _____

steps and then run _____ the growling dog and pat him on the nose!

13–14 It is _____ hot _____ play in the sun today.

15–16 The _____ hens scratched around in the dirt, hoping _____ find

some food.

Add a **clause** or **phrase** to each of these sentences.

17 On Wednesday night _____

_____ Carrie slept in her new tent.

18 Grandad _____ visits us

once a month.

19 The goats escaped _____

_____ and ate our washing!

20 William phoned Ben _____

_____ and asked if he'd like to meet in the afternoon.

4

Complete the following proverbs.

21 There is no smoke without _____ .

22 Birds of a feather flock _____ .

23 Every cloud has a silver _____ .

24 First come, first _____ .

25 More haste, less _____ .

26 When the cat's away the _____ will play.

27 Don't put all your _____ in one basket.

7

Write these statements as questions.

28 Dogs must be walked on a lead.

_____

29 Callum does all his homework in the evening.

_____

30 Tim enjoyed his birthday party.

_____

31 Sarah has gone to Spain.

_____

32 Laila hid under a cushion while watching the horror movie.

_____

33 Dean crashed his bike while trying to beat Gina home.

_____

6

Underline the **prepositions** in the following sentences.

34 They threw the ball across the playground.

35 Maria sat beside her friend Caroline.

36 They could not see beyond the hills.

37 Steven threw the ball and it went through the window.

38 Underneath the desk they found the rubber.

39 "Put the book on the table," Mum said.

40 The piano music was hidden under the pile of books.

7

Circle the words that wouldn't have been used 200 years ago.

41–47   telephone   jeans   cart   number

video   mackintosh   sheet   sun   spaceship

dog   jukebox   helicopter   candle

7

Add the missing commas to these sentences.

48–49 Danielle a freckled-faced girl skipped quietly up the road.

50–53 Huw before leaving his house for the swimming pool collected together his towel brush sunlotion and house key but forgot his swimming costume!

54–55 I jumped as high as I could flinging myself towards the lowest branch but fell collapsing on the ground from exhaustion.

8

Add a **prefix** to each of these words.

un   dis   im

56 _____ possible

57 _____ trust

58 _____ invited

59 _____ obey

60 _____ necessary

61 _____ measurable

62 _____ mortal

63 _____ named

8

Copy these sentences, adding the missing punctuation and capital letters.

64–69 time to get up rashid called to his brother

_____

70–75 gretta whispered are you awake

_____

76–82 the teacher said dont run in the corridor

_____

Form **nouns** from the **verbs** in bold to fill each gap.

83 **begin** The _____ of the book was not very exciting.

84 **invent** His _____ has proved very useful.

85 **laugh** The _____ of the crowd could be heard.

86 **solve** Tom found the _____ to the problem.

87 **speak** Before he presented the prizes, the Chairman made an interesting

_____ .

Put these words in **alphabetical order**.

mantelpiece   manager   manageable

manger   manicure   mangle

88 (1) _____   **89** (2) _____

90 (3) _____   **91** (4) _____

92 (5) _____   **93** (6) _____

Rewrite these sentences without double negatives.

94 Hayley wasn't wearing no jumper.

_____

95 Gary didn't want no breakfast.

_____

96 There wasn't no water in the stream.

_____

In each of these sentences a word is incorrect. Underline the word and rewrite it correctly.

97 The cake were all the food they had. ....

98 Neither Jack or Jill can go up the hill. ....

99 Ian and I is going to the party. ....

100 Dad gave Jim and I some apples. ....

4

100
TOTAL

Some questions will be answered in the children's own words. Answers to these questions are given in *italics*. Any answers that seem to be in line with these should be marked correct.

Paper 1

1 a person who works without being paid
2 people who count birds
3 people who search for things on the beach
4 *20,000*
5 *'you can be sure'*
6 *Royal Society for the Prevention of Cruelty to Animals*
7–8 *help with an oil disaster, help with a beached bird survey*
9 *tankers sinking close to the coast*
10 butterflies
11 melodies
12 cups
13 echoes
14 knives
15 bananas
16 puppies
17 sweets
18 girls' school
19 women's hospital
20 workers' canteen
21 children's playground
22 men's ward
23 dog's ball
24 car's wheel
25–30
    (1) probe (2) proceed
    (3) process (4) procure
    (5) produce (6) product
31–32
    Bill hit the <u>ball</u>.   He
33–34
    The young girl cut her <u>knee</u>. She
35–36
    The children in the school sang a <u>song</u>.   They
37–38
    The football team won the <u>cup</u>. They/It
39 Is the weather cold outside?
40 Are Bill and Emma going on holiday?
41 Should we leave our boots outside?

42 Does your head ache?
43 Did the dog enjoy his walk on the moor?
44 Do you ever use the old grandfather clock?
45 pressure
46 enclosure
47 failure
48 departure
49 pleasure
50 furniture
51 exposure
52 moisture
53 identical
54 postponed
55 decided
56 advanced
57 annually
58 cancelled
59 stale
60 tra**vel**
61 **des**pair
62 **com**plaint
63 **re**pel
64 but**ton**
65 post**age**
66 mol**ten**
67 sil**ver**
68 met**al**
69 Damien didn't want any food.
70 There weren't any footballs in the shed./There were no footballs in the shed.
71 There wasn't any water in the paddling pool./There was no water in the paddling pool.
72 Nina hadn't any problem with ice-skating./Nina had no problem with ice-skating.
73 Jane didn't buy any sweets from the shop.
74–79
    [six similes to be completed]
80–95
    "Where are we going?" asked a shivering Ben.
    "To the haunted house," replied Danielle.
    "I haven't got my boots on and we have to cross the stream!"

exclaimed Ben.
    "Never mind!" Danielle laughed.
96 *e.g. as*
97 *e.g. because*
98 *e.g. while*
99 *e.g. because/since*
100 *e.g. until*

Paper 2

1 *a lucky chance*
2 *go fishing*
3 *heads up*
4 *five*
5 *not really*
6 *Keith*
7 *the child or children of a particular person*
8 *He wanted the others to go exploring, it was his way of persuading them*
9 *very unjust*
10 *[answer stating what they think might have happened on the fourth day – the title 'A Crock of Gold' should be taken into consideration]*
11–12
    [two adjectives that describe a dog]
13–14
    [two adjectives that describe a chair]
15–16
    [two adjectives that describe a castle]
17–18
    [two adjectives that describe a shop]
19–20
    [two adjectives that describe shoes]
21–23
    On our holiday we visited many towns, including Bath, Bristol, Swansea, Stafford and York.
24–26
    My mum loves listening to her records of Cliff Richard, Elvis

Presley, The Beatles, Tina
Turner and Michael Jackson.

27–30

My friends are Joe, who plays
great jokes, Raju, and Zoe,
who is my best friend.

31 <u>pressure</u>
32 sub<u>div</u>ide
33 trans<u>atlantic</u>
34 dis<u>agree</u>ment
35 en<u>danger</u>ed
36 <u>magic</u>al
37 <u>frighten</u>ing
38 <u>train</u>er
39 A stitch in time – saves nine.
40 Let sleeping dogs – lie
41 Two heads are better – than one.
42 Practice – makes perfect.
43 Too many cooks – spoil the broth.
44 One good turn – deserves another.

45–50

*[second clauses added to the
beginning of sentences
provided]*

51–56

cockerel, prince, waiter, Mister,
husband, nephew

57–58

their, there

59–61

There, their, they're

62 their

63–64

They're, their

65 active
66 passive
67 passive
68 active
69 active
70 passive
71 passive
72 active
73 *e.g. contract*
74 *e.g. superior*
75 *e.g. innocent*
76 *e.g. sane*
77 *e.g. answer*
78 *e.g. multiply*
79 *e.g. hide*
80 *e.g. drop*

81–86

The wind, strong and gusty,
blew Nina's hat off.

87–92

"The film is about to start!"
yelled Anton.

93 taking
94 lamely
95 wasteful
96 sloping
97 valuable
98 wisely
99 shameful
100 believable

Paper 3

1 the world below the sea
2 salt water
3 the sea-leopard
4–5 *sluggish crawling*
6 *surface*
7 *dark-eyed/heavy-eyed*
8 *Water is the same to fish as air is to humans*
9 *[answer stating whether they think 'The world below the brine' would be a place they would like to live in and why]*
10 division
11 production
12 dictation
13 creation
14 invasion
15 resolution
16 explosion
17 lubrication

18–23

*[the completion of three
sentences, adding a connective
and clause]*

24 attentively
25 thoroughly
26 spitefully
27 longingly
28 heroically
29 patiently
30 feverishly

31–37

greenhouse, daylight,
cloudburst, watertight,
penknife, doorknob, outlook

38–54

"I think I've lost my purse,"
cried Mrs Davis. "I'd better tell
the police."

52 ceiling
53 leisure
54 eight
55 field
56 believe
57 receive
58 shield
59 seize
60 achieve
61 I am
62 do not
63 could have
64 you are
65 it is
66 they are
67 let us
68 viewpoint – *a point of view*
69 argument – *a quarrel, a reason put forward*
70 conclusion – *ending*
71 opinion – *a belief*

72–73

*[an interesting sentence using
adjectives and adverbs with the
words: cat leapt]*

74–75

*[an interesting sentence using
adjectives and adverbs with the
words: submarine sank]*

76–77

*[an interesting sentence using
adjectives and adverbs with the
words: vase smashed]*

78–79

*[an interesting sentence using
adjectives and adverbs with the
words: magazine opened]*

80–81

*[two onomatopoeic words
describing a fairground, e.g.
humming, whirring]*

82–83

*[two onomatopoeic words
describing the seaside]*

84–85

*[two onomatopoeic words
describing a zoo]*

86–87

[two onomatopoeic words describing a playground]

88 inability or disability

89 unsure or ensure or insure or assure

90 aeroplane or biplane

91 injustice

92 submarine

93 redirect or indirect or misdirect

94 displeasure

95–96

less cautious, more cautious

97–98

less dependable, more dependable

99–100

least sensible, most sensible

Paper 4

1 unhappy

2–3 rabbits, mice

4 herself

5–6 *At home she didn't grow larger and smaller and she wasn't ordered around by mice and rabbits*

7 *Alice planned to write a book about herself*

8 *She would never be an old woman*

9 *She thinks that if she never grows up she will always have to do her lessons*

10 *She had grown so much there was hardly any room for her, let alone for lesson-books*

11 kangaroos

12 atlases

13 deer

14 knives

15 mosquitoes

16 lice

17 oxen

18 chiefs

19 Tom said he'd/he would do his homework after he'd/he had watched television.

20 Mum said she would have to change her plans.

21 Dad said that he was playing cricket this evening.

22 Amanda exclaimed that she had forgotten to buy Sheena a birthday card.

23 Tony asked Tim if/whether he would like to play football.

24 Nan said that she was afraid it was time to go home.

25 present

26 future

27 past

28 past

29 present

30 present

31 past

32 *e.g. She was feeling fatigued after her hard day.*

33 *e.g. Government officials attended a meeting.*

34 *e.g. He balanced precariously on a rock.*

35 *e.g. Dad renovated the old barn.*

36 *e.g. The car nearly hit a pedestrian.*

37 *e.g. The car was submerged by the flood water.*

38 washes

39 is

40 was

41 are

42 turns

43 were

44 ate

45 drank

46 *e.g. lion*

47 *e.g. blanket*

48 *e.g. dish*

49 *e.g. cotton wool*

50 *e.g. wolf*

51 *e.g. diamonds*

52 transparent

53 separate

54 success

55 government

56 different

57 vegetables

58 thieves

59 dependable

60 library

61 sensible

62 Greek

63 studious

64 energetic

65 angelic

66 Swiss

67 triangular

68–74

Peter called, "I'm ready."

75–82

"When will we get to David's house?" Jake asked.

83–92

"Quick!" yelled Sam. "We will miss our train."

93–94

cool *e.g. (1) a low temperature (2) trendy*

95–96

trainer *e.g. (1) a type of shoe (2) a person who trains sportsmen*

97 foolish

98 graceful

99 enclosure

100 valuable

Paper 5

1 a mistake usually causes death

2 within the Arctic Circle

3 Two thousand

4 Canada

5 *to survive in the event of an emergency*

6 *by wearing them to bed, using their body heat*

7 *treated roughly by the strong cold winds*

8 *"If you survive, you've passed"*

9 *things look better*

10 *[answer stating which part of the course they would find the hardest, e.g. the cold]*

11 machinery

12 favourite

13 memory

14 sentence

15 jewellery

16 impatient

17 miserable

18 business

19–22

The girls were riding their horses.

23–25

The rabbits fled down their burrows.

26 They saved the stamps to add

30 Do it yourself
31 postage and packaging
32 care of
33 per annum
34 Brothers
35 Industrial Estate
36 Doctor

37–44
common nouns: grass, flame
collective nouns: team, gang
proper nouns: Harry,
December
abstract nouns: happiness,
opinion
45 avoided
46 improving
47 repeatedly
48 inverted
49 Recently
50 return
51 pedestrian

52–61
As **Z**oe and **R**upa slept soundly
strange things began to
happen. **A N**ight to **R**emember,
the book **R**upa had been
reading, suddenly fell open at a
page. **T**he page told the story
of a ghost which haunted the
streets of **S**kegness every
Thursday night.

62–63
[two words using the root word
– love]

64–65
[two words using the root word
– clear]

66–67
[two words using the root word
– cycle]

68–69
[two words using the root word
– pay]
70 France
71 China
72 Pakistan
73 Sweden
74 Australia
75 Wales
76 Jamaica

77–78
Wes thought that he must
have been dreaming

79–80
My Dad collapsed into his
chair, because the run had
exhausted him!

81–82
The picture fell from the wall,
glass smashing everywhere.

83–84
Judy wondered whether the
book might be useful for her
project.

85 *in answer to your letter*
86 *a form can be got from*
87 *if you want to come*
88 *we are letting you know*

89–94
"Where is Jess?" moaned Dad.
"We really need to get going or
we will miss our ferry." / "She is
coming. I can hear her racing
down the stairs," replied Mum.
/ "About time too!" continued
Dad. / As Jess climbed into the
car Mum enquired, "Have you
got your coat?" / "Oops . . .
shall I go and get it?" Jess
asked. / "Yes, and be VERY
quick," Dad almost shouted.
"I'm losing my patience!" /
"Sorry," she called as she flew
into the house.

95 (3)
96 (2)
97 (1)
98 (3)
99 (1)
100 (2)

Paper 6

1 Holland
2 more than 2 years
3 half an hour
4 *the Van Daan family*
5 *She was frightened and wanted*
something to hold
6 *the extreme point*
7 *subsided*
8 *She was too frightened to think*
about food

9 *[answer stating what Anne*
might have had in her 'escape
bag']

10–12
to, two, to

13–14
too, to

15–16
two, to

17–20
[four clauses or phrases added
to part sentences]
21 fire
22 together
23 lining
24 served
25 speed
26 mice
27 eggs
28 Must dogs be walked on a
lead?/Should dogs be walked
on a lead?
29 Does Callum do all his
homework in the evening?
30 Did Tim enjoy his birthday
party?
31 Has Sarah gone to Spain?
32 Did Laila hide under a cushion
while watching the horror
movie?
33 Did Dean crash his bike while
trying to beat Gina home?
34 across
35 beside
36 beyond
37 through
38 Underneath
39 on
40 under

41–47
telephone, jeans, video,
mackintosh, spaceship,
jukebox, helicopter

48–49
Danielle, a freckled-faced girl,
skipped quietly up the road.

50–53
Huw, before leaving his house
for the swimming pool,
collected together his towel,
brush, sunlotion and house key
but forgot his swimming
costume!

I jumped as high as I could, flinging myself towards the lowest branch, but fell collapsing on the ground from exhaustion.

56 impossible
57 distrust
58 uninvited
59 disobey
60 unnecessary
61 immeasurable
62 immortal
63 unnamed

64–69

"Time to get up," Rashid called to his brother.

70–75

Gretta whispered, "Are you awake?"

76–82

The teacher said, "Don't run in the corridor."

83 beginning
84 invention
85 laughter
86 solution
87 speech
88 manageable
89 manager
90 manger
91 mangle
92 manicure
93 mantelpiece
94 Hayley wasn't wearing a jumper.
95 Gary didn't want breakfast./Gary didn't want any breakfast.
96 There wasn't any water in the stream./There was no water in the stream.
97 <u>were</u> – was
98 <u>or</u> – nor
99 <u>is</u> – are
100 <u>I</u> – me

Paper 7

1 no
2 the church organist
3 fairy music

---

4 *not very well*
5 unlatched
6 *dizzy and sick*
7 *harp*
8 *reluctantly*
9 *compelled to go on*
10 *the narrator's eyes got used to the darkness*
11 *a traveller in time*
12 caught
13 lay
14 fought
15 went
16 hid
17 shrank
18 crept
19 noticeable
20 sensible
21 advisable
22 responsible
23 honourable
24 reasonable
25 imaginable
26 forcible
27 active
28 passive
29 passive
30 active
31 active
32 active
33 passive
34 wriggle
35 hymn
36 knock
37 limb
38 whisker
39 autumn
40 knelt
41 bomb
42 please turn over
43 United States of America
44 Member of Parliament or Military Police
45 North West
46 millilitres or mile
47 Department
48 as soon as possible
49 *e.g. although*
50 *e.g. until*
51 *e.g. if*
52 *e.g. whether*
53 *e.g. as/because*
54 *e.g. but*

---

friend, companion, secretary, giant, orphan, guest, cousin

62 gracefully
63 attentively
64 heavily
65 brightly
66 silently
67 somehow
68 often
69 fluently

70–75

[a passage containing the six stated words arguing the case for or against wearing school uniform]

76 happily
77 fried
78 hurrying
79 noisily
80 worried
81 crying

82–100

"Can someone answer the phone?" yelled Mum.
"I'll get it," called Sam.
All was quiet when suddenly Sam screamed, "We've won a holiday!"

Paper 8

1 It is not easy to pronounce
2–3 Irving, Tree
4–5 *he is shabby and thin*
6 *Firefrorefiddle, the Fiend of the Fell*
7 *an hour*
8 *The audience always enjoyed his performances*
9 *Yes, he meets friends and tells them stories about his past*
10 *without preparation talk back to the audience*
11 blind
12 easy
13 chirpy
14 tough
15 dry
16 fit
17 sober
18 quiet

19 are
20 was
21 are
22 was
23 is
24 are
25 were
26 false
27 true
28 false
29 true
30 true
31 false
32 false
33 true

34–38
[clauses with a conjunction added to the main clauses]

39 roofs
40 axes
41 flutes
42 shelves
43 halves
44 pianos
45 Kate called urgently to me to get down./Kate called urgently to me that I should get down.
46 Dad mumbled that there was a knock at the door.
47 Joe urged that we should take Clawdie to the vet.
48 The farmer called that the cows could be let into the field.
49 incorrect
50 unaware
51 unselfish
52 disrespect
53 improbable
54 disobedient
55 disconnect
56 distrust or mistrust

57–62
"Time you were in bed," said Nicky, the babysitter. / "Do we have to?" asked Ben. "I'm not at all tired!" / "Your dad said bed at 8 o'clock, I'm afraid." / "But he wouldn't know," Alice objected. / "No, he wouldn't, if you didn't tell him," confirmed Ben. / "If you go to bed now, you can have your light on in your rooms for another hour,"

Nicky suggested. / "What a good idea!" Alice agreed. "We could read a book."

63 press
64 height
65 collapse
66 eat
67 decorate
68 doubt
69 form
70 state

71–76
[two sentences, each with three commas]

77–86
[table of nouns appropriately filled in]

87–93
any seven of: stonework, kneecap, firework, fireweed, blackhead, blackcap, blackmail, horseshoe, seaweed, crossroads

94 villain
95 syllabus
96 deceive
97 pavilion
98 puncture
99 generous
100 drawing

Paper 9

1 marmoset
2 drawer
3 six o'clock exactly
4 *being left for an afternoon*
5 *half an hour or so*
6 *when he was feeling affectionate*
7 *e.g. stare*
8 *regal*
9 *unwillingly*
10 *yes, he had many human characteristics*
11 to advertise
12 to depart
13 to fly
14 to applaud
15 to deliver
16 to injure
17 to conclude
18 the girls' hats

19 the wasp's sting
20 Tess's home
21 the children's books
22 his friend's bike
23 the lion's mane
24 the teacher's scissors

25–36
[an adjective and a verb added to the gaps in the sentences]

37 unfurnished – *without furniture*
38 dejected – *in low spirits*
39 courteous – *polite*
40 spectator – *a person who watches*
41 assisted – *helped*
42 endeavour – *to try*
43 resemble – *to look like*
44 practice
45 practise
46 principal
47 principle
48 their
49 there
50 course
51 coarse
52 omelette
53 minnow
54 shallow
55 flannel
56 arrive
57 quarrel
58 goggle
59 struggle
60 S   61 C   62 Q   63 Q
64 S   65 Q   66 C   67 S
68 lump of lead – head
69 skin and blister – sister
70 frog and toad – road
71 mince pies – eyes
72 sugar and honey – money
73 dog and bone – telephone
74 Barnet Fair – hair
75 *e.g. shall, might, will, may*
76 *e.g. will, might*
77 *e.g. won't, shan't*
78 *e.g. would, should*
79 *e.g. will, might*
80 annually
81 frequently
82 regretted
83 decided
84 audience
85 congregation

86 occasionally
87 cleverest
88 poorest
89 worst
90 ugliest
91 reddest
92 most generous
93 best
94 most curious
95–100
owlet, duckling, piglet, lambkin, statuette, booklet

Paper 10

1 deliberate destruction
2 someone lower in rank
3 using anything which is handy
4–7 *practise a slouch, alter shape of face, darken or bleach skin, dye hair*
8 *as darkness is used as a cover*
9 *very skilful*
10–12
e.g. patience, practicality, bravery, adaptability
13 of
14 to
15 with
16 of
17 of
18 between
19 on
20 v**e**getable
21 lag**oo**n
22 **e**xtra
23 regr**e**ttable
24 **e**ffort
25 fr**ee**dom
26 **i**nterest
27 t**e**mperature
28–37
"I will never believe it though," replied old Jeremiah. "Never."
38 evidence – *a reason for believing something*
39 conclusion – *ending*
40 viewpoint – *a point of view*
41 summary – *main points about something*
42 furthermore – *in addition*
43–44
"No, I'm not going to the park

after school," stated Tracy.
45–46
Today, without realising it, James was going to have the best day of his life.
47 Mandy forgot the milk, the bread and the tin of sweetcorn!
48 Sarah stopped, looked round and listened.
49–50
"Yes, it's time to eat the party food," called Mum.
51 *e.g. swarm*
52 *e.g. happily, almost*
53 *e.g. but*
54 *e.g. he*
55 *e.g. ran*
56 *e.g. brown*
57 *e.g. happiness*
58 exact
59 excellent
60 extend
61 extinction
62 extra
63 extract
64–65
e.g. overall, overboard
66–67
e.g. before, behead, bespatter
68–69
e.g. outside, outline
70–71
e.g. underarm, underwear
72–81
"Did you see the newspaper this morning?" asked Tim.
"Yes," replied Nathan.
As he rushed past the kitchen table he stopped himself to read the headline, 'Banbury School flooded'. It reminded him of a book he'd read called Disasters at School.
82–86
[the completion of five sentences]
87 picture
88 possession
89 February
90 mischief
91 describe
92 barbecue
93 Saturday

94 opposite
95–100
[the completion of six metaphors]

Paper 11

1 used sparingly
2 in the course of several days
3 it was a very long time
4 *They knew their food would not last for ever*
5 *Their water was carried in skins*
6–8 *fast, strong, black*
9 *not to get wet*
10 *[answer stating how they would cross the stream without getting wet]*
11–17
[seven synonyms for the word 'said', e.g. talked, muttered, whispered, shouted]
18 *[an adjectival phrase about a ball]*
19 *[an adjectival phrase about a horse]*
20 *[an adjectival phrase about an igloo]*
21 *[an adjectival phrase about a sandwich]*
22 *[an adjectival phrase about the sun]*
23 *[an adjectival phrase about a story]*
24 they're
25 should've
26 I've
27 we'll
28 there's
29 won't
30 you're
31 don't
32 acquaintance
33 imagination
34 pollution
35 competitor
36 restraint
37 employer
38 detective
39 bribery
40 dictionary
41 nursery
42 memory

43 brewery
44 victory
45 discovery
46 ordinary
47 salary
48 A form needs to be obtained from the Post Office.
You will be notified shortly.
Please respond promptly.
The tenant has been informed of the decision.
No fishing in the pond.
No running by the swimming pool.

54–55
daughter, niece

56–57
headmistress, women

58–59
princess, heroine

60–61
aunt, her

62–64
is, is, are

65–69
was, were, was, were, were

70–73
[a subordinate clause to be added to each main clause provided]

74 torpedo
75 calf
76 valley
77 sheep
78 mouse
79 battery
80 fox
81 olive

82–94
"I can hear something," whispered Sandra.
"So can I," confirmed Jess.
"What could it be?"

95–96
did, done

97 done
98 did
99 pencil case
100 computer disk

Paper 12

1–2 Charlotte, Wilbur

3 autumn
4 *because she was rather quiet*
5 *the ice will melt on the pond*
6 *spring and summer will return*
7 *they get taken to the market and sold*
8 *because spiders trap and eat flies*
9 [answer stating whether friends are important and why]
10 answer
11 wreck
12 castle
13 tongue
14 lamb
15 design
16 rhubarb
17 white
18 walk
19 before
20 her
21 and
22 he
23 patiently
24 drawer
25 I can see Paul hiding behind the bench.
26 The Fish and Chip shop is open.
27 The homework is due in on Monday
28 The tree is safe to climb on.
29 We can go out and play in the snow.
30 Bring your coats./We did bring our coats/We brought our coats.
31 agreement
32 alphabetical
33 impersonal
34 onlooker
35 returned
36 submerge
37 instruction
38 defrosted
39 active
40 passive
41 active
42 passive
43 passive
44 active
45 lubricate – *to oil something so that it moves easily*

46 minimum – *the smallest quantity*
47 summit – *the highest point*
48 abbreviate – *to shorten*
49 obedient – *doing what you are told*
50 resolve – *to sort out / to decide to do something*
51 proceed – *to go forward*
52 careless
53 hairy
54 painless
55 starless
56 useless
57 cloudy

58–80
As Rudi jumped into the pool Alice screamed. She hated water on her face though she loved playing on the inflatables. That is why she had wanted a swimming birthday party.
"Can you stop jumping near me, please?" asked Alice, as water dripped from her nose.
"If I have to," laughed Rudi.

81 e-mail – *electronic mail*
82 newscast – *news broadcast*
83 heliport – *helicopter airport*
84 cheeseburger – *cheese hamburger*
85 smog – *smoke and fog*

86–87
[child's own phrase or clause added to sentences provided]

88 David wasn't afraid.
89 Gina copied Helen's homework.

90–91
We're going to get to Uncle Matt's house before it is dark.

92 We could hear the puppies' wails.
93 What's the problem?

94–95
Jack's Mum wouldn't let him play on his bike.

96 NZ
97 RSPB
98 SOS
99 UAE
100 RSA

Paper 7

The church door was shut and there was never a glimmer of candlelight although it was nearly dark with the pouring rain. I walked slowly, dragging back, yet constrained to move forward as the music came in elvish sweetness. Mrs Pluck never played like that; her music was faltering and broken except when she thumped out a well-known hymn. This was no hymn, it wasn't sacred music at all, and for that I was glad, but it was unearthly and fairy, as if the wind had come down to earth to play a harp of willow boughs. It was unlike anything I had ever heard, and I stood in the church porch sheltering from the rain, listening, hesitating. I felt dizzy and sick and I began to tremble. I unlatched the great door and slowly pushed it open. The church was in pitch darkness as if it were the middle of the night. The blackness lightened and I could distinguish a figure crouched by the font. It was Arabella with a small harp in her hands.

From *A Traveller in Time* by Alison Uttley

Underline the right answers.

1 Was it night time?
(yes, no, we are not told)

2 Who was Mrs Pluck?
(a school teacher, the church organist, someone visiting the church)

3 What was the music like?
(fairy music, church music, pop music, folk music)

3

Answer these questions.

4 How well did Mrs Pluck play the organ?

5 In the passage find the word used for 'opened'.

_____

6 How did the music make the listener feel?

_____

7 What instrument was being played?

_____

8 What do you think 'dragging back' means?

_____

9 What do you think 'constrained to move forward' means?

_____

10 Why do you think 'the blackness lightened' once the narrator was inside the church?

_____

11 Who do you think Arabella was?

_____

8

Change the word in bold into the **past tense**.

12 **catch**   I _____ the last bus home.

13 **lie**   I _____ in bed reading for about an hour.

14 **fight**   The boys _____ against the gang from the High Street.

15 **go**   We _____ to London every Easter.

16 **hide**   They _____ in the cupboard under the stairs.

17 **shrink**   When I washed my jumper it _____.

18 **creep**   They made her jump as they _____ up behind her.

7

Write each of these words with either the *able* or *ible* **suffix**. Don't forget any necessary spelling changes.

19 notice   _____   20 sense   _____

21 advise   _____   22 response _____

23 honour   _____   24 reason   _____

25 imagine   _____   26 force   _____

8

34

State whether each of these sentences has an *active* or *passive* **verb**.

27 Tammy caught measles. _____

28 Daniel was frightened by the noise. _____

29 The mouse was seized with fear on seeing the cat. _____

30 Bola hit his head. _____

31 The sweets fell out of the bag. _____

32 The lorry damaged the gate. _____

33 Jenny was bitten by the big dog. _____ `7`

Rewrite each word, adding the missing silent letter so that each word is spelt correctly.

34 riggle _____   35 hym _____

36 nock _____   37 lim _____

38 wisker _____   39 autum _____

40 nelt _____   41 bom _____ `8`

Write the following **abbreviations** in full.

42 PTO _____

43 USA _____

44 MP _____

45 NW _____

46 ml _____

47 Dept. _____

48 a.s.a.p. _____ `7`

Add a **conjunction** to each sentence.

49 The sun was warm _____ it was December.

50 The children played in the pool _____ the weather grew cold and windy.

51 I don't have to do it _____ I don't want to.

52 He did not know _____ his friend wanted to go swimming.

53 She was sent home _____ she was not well.

54 I want to go to Italy _____ I cannot afford to. `6`

Underline any word which applies to both males and females.

55–61   girl   friend   uncle   niece   vixen   companion

secretary   giant   orphan   aunt   guest   cousin

Choose an **adverb** which would best describe each **verb**.

somehow   brightly   often

gracefully   heavily   silently   attentively   fluently

62 The ballerina danced _____ .

63 The class listened _____ .

64 The rain beat _____ .

65 The sun shone _____ .

66 The burglar crept _____ .

67 The goats _____ managed to escape from their pen.

68 The boys _____ play snooker.

69 The woman spoke Spanish _____ .

Write the following six words in a passage that argues the case for or against the wearing of school uniform.

70–75   conclusion   opinion   although   believe

discussion   besides

_____

_____

_____

_____

Add the **suffixes** to these words ending in y. Don't forget any necessary spelling changes.

76 happy + ly   _____

77 fry + ed   _____

78 hurry + ing _____

79 noisy + ly _____

80 worry + ed _____

81 cry + ing _____

Rewrite this passage correctly.

82–100 can someone answer the phone yelled mum
I'll get it called sam
all was quiet when suddenly sam screamed weve won a holiday

_____

_____

_____

_____

_____

_____

Paper 8

Gus is the Cat at the Theatre Door.
His name, as I ought to have told you before,
Is really Asparagus. That's such a fuss
To pronounce, that we usually call him just Gus.
His coat's very shabby, he's thin as a rake,
And he suffers from palsy that makes his paw shake.
Yet he was, in his youth, quite the smartest of Cats –
But no longer a terror to mice and to rats.
For he isn't the Cat that he was in his prime;
Though his name was quite famous, he says, in its time.
And whenever he joins his friends at their club
(Which takes place at the back of the neighbouring pub)
He loves to regale them, if someone else pays,
With anecdotes drawn from his palmiest days.
For once he was a Star of the highest degree –
He has acted with Irving, he's acted with Tree,
And he likes to relate his success on the Halls,
Where the Gallery once gave him seven cat-calls.
But his grandest creation, as he loves to tell,
Was Firefrorefiddle, the Fiend of the Fell.

"I have played," so he says, "every possible part,
And I used to know seventy speeches by heart.
I'd extemporise back-chat, I knew how to gag,
And I knew how to let the cat out of the bag.
I knew how to act with my back and my tail;
With an hour of rehearsal, I never could fail.
I'd a voice that would soften the hardest of hearts,
Whether I took the lead, or in character parts.
I have sat by the bedside of poor Little Nell;
When the Curfew was rung, then I swung on the bell.
In the Pantomime season I never fell flat,
And once I understudied Dick Whittington's Cat.
But my grandest creation, as history will tell,
Was Firefrorefiddle, the Fiend of the Fell."

From 'Gus the Theatre Cat' by T S Eliot

Underline the right answers.

1 Why isn't Gus called Asparagus, even though it is his name?
(It is not easy to pronounce, It is a silly name, He doesn't like asparagus)

2–3 Which two actors are mentioned?
(Irving, Tree, Little Nell, Dick Whittington)

`3`

Answer these questions.

4–5 What does Gus look like now?

_____

6 What was the most important part Gus ever played?

_____

7 How long did Gus need for rehearsal?

_____

8 What do you think the poet means by 'he never fell flat'?

_____

9 Do you think Gus is now a popular cat? Why?

_____

10 What do you think 'extemporise back-chat' means?

_____

`7`

Complete the following **similes**.

11 As _____ as a bat.

12 As _____ as pie.

13 As _____ as a cricket.

14 As _____ as leather.

15 As _____ as dust.

16 As _____ as a fiddle.

17 As _____ as a judge.

18 As _____ as a mouse.

`8`

Underline the correct **verb** form in each sentence.

19   There (is/are) many bags to choose from.

20   He (was/were) running when he slipped into the puddle.

21   They (is/are) going to swim the Channel.

22   It (was/were) time to go home.

23   When (is/are) Greg arriving?

24   You (is/are) very tired, aren't you?

25   Susan's sisters (was/were) much older than her.

7

We are interrupting our programmes to give you an urgent police message. At about 10 a.m. today some dangerous drugs were stolen from a doctor's blue Renault car which was parked in the High Street, Lowby. The drugs look like pink sweets, and we are told that they might be very dangerous, particularly if swallowed by children. If anyone can help the police, then please telephone Lowby 123456 as soon as possible.

Write *true* or *false* next to each statement.

26   This notice appeared in a newspaper.   _____

27   The doctor's car was parked in the High Street this morning.   _____

28   The drugs are not dangerous if taken by adults.   _____

29   The drugs look like sweets.   _____

30   This announcement was made on television or radio or both.   _____

31   The police want to interview the doctor.   _____

32   The police are in a hurry as the doctor shouldn't have been in the High Street.   _____

33   It is urgent because people may have swallowed the drugs.   _____

8

Add a **clause** with a **conjunction** to each of these **main clauses**.

34   The dog sprinted through the park _____

_____

35   David took great care _____

_____

40

36 The twins queued for hours _____

_____

37 Karen kicked the football with all her might _____

_____

38 At last Kofi handed his story to his teacher _____

_____

5

Write the **plural** forms of these words.

39 roof _____ **40** axe _____

41 flute _____ **42** shelf _____

43 half _____ **44** piano _____

6

Write these sentences as **reported speech**.

45 "Get down from there," Kate called urgently to me.

_____

46 "There's a knock at the door," mumbled Dad.

_____

47 "We should take Clawdie to the vet," Joe urged.

_____

48 "Let the cows into the field," the farmer called.

_____

4

Write an **antonym** for each of these words by adding a **prefix**.

49 correct _____ **50** aware _____

51 selfish _____ **52** respect _____

53 probable _____ **54** obedient _____

55 connect _____ **56** trust _____

8

Draw a line (/) every time a new line should have been started in the following dialogue.

57–62 "Time you were in bed," said Nicky, the babysitter. "Do we have to?" asked Ben. "I'm not at all tired!" "Your dad said bed at 8 o'clock, I'm afraid." "But he wouldn't know," Alice objected. "No, he wouldn't, if you didn't tell him," confirmed Ben. "If you go to bed now, you can have your light on in your rooms for another hour," Nicky suggested. "What a good idea!" Alice agreed. "We could read a book."

6

Write the **root word** in each word.

63	pressure _____	64	heightened _____
65	collapsible _____	66	eaten _____
67	decoration _____	68	doubtful _____
69	transform _____	70	statement _____

8

Write two sentences, each with three commas.

71–73

_____

_____

_____

74–76

_____

_____

_____

6

Fill the gaps in the table with appropriate **nouns**.

77–86

Common nouns	Proper nouns	Collective nouns	Abstract nouns

10

42

Using a word from each column write seven compound words.

87–93

stone	head
knee	shoe
fire	cap
black	weed
horse	roads
sea	work
cross	mail

_____   _____   _____

_____   _____   _____

_____

7

The words below are wrongly spelt. Rewrite them correctly.

94 villan   _____

95 sylabus   _____

96 decieve   _____

97 pavillion   _____

98 punture   _____

99 genrous   _____

100 drawring   _____

7

100
TOTAL

Paper 9

We had to be ready to put him to bed at six o'clock sharp, and if we were late he would stalk furiously up and down outside his drawer, his fur standing on end with rage. We had to learn not to slam doors shut, without first looking to see if Pavlo was sitting on top, because, for some reason, he liked to sit on doors and meditate. But our worst crime, according to him, was when we went out and left him for an afternoon. When we returned he would leave us in no doubt as to his feelings on the subject; we would be in disgrace. He would turn his back on us in disgust when we tried to talk to him; he would go and sit in a corner and glower at us, his little face screwed up into a scowl. After half an hour or so he would, very reluctantly, forgive us and with regal condescension accept a lump of sugar and some warm milk before retiring to bed. The marmoset's moods were most human, for he would scowl and mutter at you when he felt bad tempered, and, very probably, try to give you a nip. When he was feeling affectionate, however, he would approach you with a loving expression on his face, poking his tongue out and in rapidly, smacking his lips, climb on to your shoulder and give your ear a series of passionate nibbles.

From *Portrait of Pavlo* by Gerald Durrell

Underline the right answers.

1   Pavlo was a (human being, dog, marmoset, baboon).

2   Pavlo slept in a (bed, drawer, nest, corner).

3   'Six o'clock sharp' means (just before six, just after six, about six, six o'clock exactly).

44

Answer these questions.

4 What did Pavlo most dislike?

_____

5 How long did Pavlo's moods usually last?

_____

6 When did Pavlo poke his tongue out?

_____

7 Write a synonym for the word 'glower'.

_____

8 Write the word from the passage that means 'like a king'.

_____

9 What do you think 'reluctantly' means?

_____

10 Do you think Pavlo was intelligent? Why?

_____

Change each of the **nouns** in bold to the infinitive of the **verb**.

e.g.   He was good at **multiplication**.   _to multiply_

11 She saw the **advertisement** on television.   _____

12 The **departure** of the train was delayed.   _____

13 The '**Flight** of the Bumble Bee' is a popular piece of music.   _____

14 The **applause** lasted for several minutes.   _____

15 The **delivery** of the mail is erratic on the island.   _____

16 Fortunately the **injury** was not serious.   _____

17 The story reached an interesting **conclusion**.   _____

Write these in the possessive case, i.e. with an apostrophe.

e.g.   the bone of the dog   _the dog's bone_

18 the hats of the girls   _____

19 the sting of the wasp _____

20 the home of Tess _____

21 the books of the children _____

22 the bike of his friend _____

23 the mane of the lion _____

24 the scissors of the teacher _____ | 7. |

Add an **adjective** and **verb** to complete each sentence.

25–28 The girl _____ towards the _____ horse.

29–32 The _____ kite _____ in the sky.

33–36 Monty, the dog, _____ towards the _____ man. | 12 |

Write a **definition** for each of these words.

37 unfurnished _____

38 dejected _____

39 courteous _____

40 spectator _____

41 assisted _____

42 endeavour _____

43 resemble _____ | 7 |

Underline the correct **homophone**.

44 The doctor's (practise, practice) is in Warwick Road.

45 They (practise, practice) their judo.

46 The (principal, principle) of the college had taught abroad.

47 It was a matter of (principal, principle) that he should write the letter.

48 Where is (their, there) rabbit?

49 I put it over (their, there).

50 The (coarse, course) of the river meanders through the field.

51 The material she used was very (coarse, course). | 8 |

Add the correct double letters to create a word.

rr   ll   tt   nn   gg

52 omle____e   **53** mi____ow

54 sha____ow   **55** fla____el

56 a____ive   **57** qua____el

58 go____le   **59** stru____le

8

What are the following: statements, questions or commands?
Write *S* for a statement, *Q* for a question and *C* for a command.

60 The United Kingdom has an equable climate   _____

61 Bring me the scissors   _____

62 Did you put it on the table   _____

63 What is the answer   _____

64 Deciduous trees lose their leaves in winter   _____

65 Are evergreen trees always green   _____

66 Put on your shoes   _____

67 The dog barked loudly   _____

8

Match, with a line, the Cockney rhyming slang with its meaning.

68 lump of lead   hair

69 skin and blister   telephone

70 frog and toad   head

71 mince pies   money

72 sugar and honey   road

73 dog and bone   eyes

74 Barnet Fair   sister

7

Add a suitable helper **verb** to each of these **conditional** sentences (when one thing depends on something else).

75 I _____ ring when I get home if my mum lets me.

76 Should it rain, we _____ buy an umbrella.

77 I _____ do anything unless I hear from you.

78 I _____ like to go swimming, providing it doesn't rain.

79 Your purse _____ be stolen if you leave the car unlocked.

Write a **synonym** for the words in bold.

80 They went on holiday **each year**.   _____

81 Sue goes there quite **often**.   _____

82 She **was sorry** that she had been naughty.   _____

83 Tom **made up his mind** to go to the cinema.   _____

84 The **people who had been watching** clapped loudly
    when the play ended.   _____

85 The **people at the church service** listened attentively
    to the vicar's sermon.   _____

86 **Now and then** we go to the cinema.   _____

Write the **superlative** form of the **adjective** on the left.

87 **clever**   That is the _____ answer of all.

88 **poor**   The _____ families live there.

89 **bad**   They reported the _____ gale for ten years.

90 **ugly**   She was the _____ of the sisters.

91 **red**   My apple is the _____ one I have ever seen.

92 **generous** Mum is the _____ person I know.

93 **good**   That is the _____ conker I have played with.

94 **curious**   Alice thought it was the _____ thing she had ever seen.

Underline the **diminutives**.

95–100   model   bull   owlet   fireplace   lioness

                duckling   hare   gander   piglet   dog

                lambkin   magazine   statuette   booklet

Paper 10

Sabotage is an essential part of espionage. The spy must know a great deal about demolition charges and booby traps. And he must be able to fit such things in the dark.

He is trained in the art of burglary, using simple tools or, better still, improvisation. He must be adept in fashioning and using skeleton keys and pick-locks.

He must not only know the tools of his trade; he must be able to teach their use to others. Some spies operate single-handed, others are part of an organisation. The leader of the group must be able to brief his subordinates – who may be untrained local people.

He must be expert at unarmed combat. A shot attracts attention – the spy must be trained to kill silently.

He is even taught some details of disguise; not wigs and whiskers, which are rather too obvious, but small changes which could deceive an observer. He could appear to be about two inches shorter by practising a slouch. He can alter the shape of his face temporarily by stuffing slices of apple or potato under his cheeks. There are solutions which will darken his skin or bleach it. The dyeing of his hair will effect a considerable change in his appearance.

From *Spy School* by Bernard Newman

Underline the right answers.

1   'Sabotage' is (deliberate destruction, accidental damage, a hidden danger).

2   A 'subordinate' is (a fellow worker, someone in charge, someone lower in rank).

3 'Improvisation' is (using a complicated machine, using anything which is handy, having improved tools).

3

Answer these questions.

4–7 List the four details of disguise suggested in the passage.

_____

_____

_____

_____

8 Why do you think a spy must be able to work in the dark?

_____

9 What do you think the word 'adept' means?

_____

10–12 Name three qualities a spy would need.

_____

_____

9

In each space write the correct **preposition**.

13 I am beginning to despair _____ Jane ever doing better work.

14 That cake is similar _____ one that Dad makes.

15 Mr Bell was very angry _____ Tom when he broke the window.

16 Miss Jones said that she did not approve _____ the way I did my hair.

17 David said that he did not like being accused _____ being unkind.

18 The prize money is being divided _____ Jonathan and his brother.

19 Mum said that she could rely _____ me to do the shopping.

7

Underline the *stressed vowel* sound in each word.

20 v e g e t a b l e   **21** l a g o o n   **22** e x t r a

23 r e g r e t t a b l e   **24** e f f o r t   **25** f r e e d o m

26 i n t e r e s t   **27** t e m p e r a t u r e

8

Punctuate this.

28–37 i will never believe it though replied old jeremiah never

_____

_____

10

Write a **definition** for each of these words.

38 evidence _____

39 conclusion _____

40 viewpoint _____

41 summary _____

42 furthermore _____

5

Add the missing commas to these sentences.

43–44 "No I'm not going to the park after school" stated Tracy.

45–46 Today without realising it James was going to have the best day of his life.

47 Mandy forgot the milk the bread and the tin of sweetcorn!

48 Sarah stopped looked round and listened.

49–50 "Yes it's time to eat the party food" called Mum.

8

Write an example of each.

51 **collective noun** _____

52 **adverb** _____

53 **conjunction** _____

54 **pronoun** _____

55 **verb** _____

56 **adjective** _____

57 **abstract noun** _____

7

Write these words in **alphabetical order**.

excellent   extinction   extra   extract   exact   extend

58 (1) _____   **59** (2) _____

60 (3) _____   **61** (4) _____

62 (5) _____   **63** (6) _____

`6`

Write two words that begin with each of these **prefixes**.

64–65 **over**   _____   _____

66–67 **be**   _____   _____

68–69 **out**   _____   _____

70–71 **under**   _____   _____

`8`

Circle the letters in this passage that should be capitals.

72–81 "did you see the newspaper this morning?" asked tim. "yes," replied nathan.

as he rushed past the kitchen table he stopped himself to read the headline, 'banbury school flooded'. it reminded him of a book he'd read called disasters at school.

`10`

Complete these as **complex sentences**. Use **conjunctions** such as: when, before, after, because. Do not use: and, but, so, or.

82 Darius fell in a puddle _____

_____

83 The children wrapped up well _____

_____

84 Meena couldn't find what she wanted on the internet _____

_____

85 Cleo, the cat, snuggled up next to the fire _____

_____

86 The children loved the fancy dress party _____

`5`

_____

Write each of these words correctly.

87 piture _____

88 posession _____

89 Febuary _____

90 mischeif _____

91 discribe _____

92 barbeque _____

93 Saterday _____

94 oppisite _____

Complete each sentence as a **metaphor**.

95 The snow is _____

96 The rain fell _____

97 The sky was _____

98 The grass _____

99 The sun _____

100 The cows _____

Paper 11

All this went on for what seemed to the hobbit ages upon ages; and he was always hungry, for they were extremely careful with their provisions. Even so, as days followed days, and still the forest seemed just the same, they began to get anxious. The food would not last for ever: it was in fact already beginning to get low. They tried shooting at the squirrels, and they wasted many arrows before they managed to bring one down on the path. But when they roasted it, it proved horrible to taste, and they shot no more squirrels.

They were thirsty too, for they had none too much water, and in all the time they had seen neither spring nor stream. This was their state when one day they found their path blocked by running water. It flowed fast and strong but not very wide right across the way, and it was black, or looked it in the gloom. It was well that Beorn had warned them against it, or they would have drunk from it, whatever its colour, and filled some of their emptied skins at its banks. As it was, they only thought of how to cross it without wetting themselves in the water.

From *The Hobbit* by J R R Tolkien

Underline the right answers.

1 Their provisions were (guarded carefully, used sparingly, not eaten at all).

2 'Days followed days' means (it was constant daylight, they did not notice the nights, in the course of several days).

3 'Ages upon ages' means (an everlasting time, it was a very long time, they added their ages together).

3

Answer these questions.

4 Why were they beginning to get anxious?

_____

5 How did they carry their water?

_____

6–8 Write three words that are used to describe the stream.

_____   _____   _____

9 What did they have to be very careful about when crossing the stream?

_____

10 If you were the Hobbit, how do you think you would cross the stream?

_____

7

Write seven **synonyms** for the word *said*.

11–17 _____   _____   _____

_____   _____   _____

_____

7

Write an **adjectival phrase** about each of these nouns.

18 a ball _____

19 a horse _____

54

20	an igloo	_____	
21	a sandwich	_____	
22	the sun	_____	
23	a story	_____	**6**

Write the **contraction** for each of these.

24	they are	_____	25	should have	_____
26	I have	_____	27	we will	_____
28	there is	_____	29	will not	_____
30	you are	_____	31	do not	_____ **8**

Form a **noun** from each of the **verbs** in bold.

32	**acquaint**	The girl made my _____ at the bus stop.
33	**imagine**	She used her _____ to write an excellent story.
34	**pollute**	The _____ of the river was scandalous.
35	**compete**	One _____ was late for the start of the race.
36	**restrain**	Dad acted with _____ though he was boiling with rage.
37	**employ**	I work for Mr Smith, who is a very kind _____ .
38	**detect**	The _____ solved the crime.

7

Add *ary*, *ery* or *ory* to complete each word.

39	brib_____	40	diction_____	41	nurs_____
42	mem_____	43	brew_____	44	vict_____
45	discov_____	46	ordin_____	47	sal_____

9

Underline the sentences that use official-type language.

48–53   A form needs to be obtained from the Post Office.

You will be notified shortly.

Thanks for your letter; it was great to hear from you.

Please respond promptly.

The tenant has been informed of the decision.

Please can I ride my bike to the shop?

No fishing in the pond.

Tony handed the jacket he found to Lost Property.

No running by the swimming pool.

Change the words in bold into their feminine form.

54–55 My (**son**) _____ showed the book to my (**nephew**) _____.

56–57 The (**headmaster**) _____ interviewed the two (**men**) _____.

58–59 The (**prince**) _____ presented the medal to the (**hero**) _____.

60–61 Sam's (**uncle**) _____ always made (**him**) _____ laugh.

8

Add *is* or *are* in each gap to make the passage correct.

62–64 Dan _____ the tallest boy in the school. Everyone _____

quite envious of him. They _____ nowhere near as tall.

3

Add *was* or *were* in each gap to make the passage correct.

65–69 There _____ a firework party on New Year's Eve.

There _____ hundreds of people and when the clock

_____ about to strike midnight everyone held hands and

counted down the seconds. They _____ very excited – the

fireworks _____ about to be lit.

5

Add a **subordinate clause** to each of these **main clauses** using the **conjunctions** given in bold.

70 after The dog jumped into the water _____

_____

71 until Ruth slept peacefully in her bed _____

_____

72 because Tanya puzzled over her homework _____

_____

73 before A letter arrived for Ahmed _____

4

_____

Write the **singular** form of each word.

74 torpedoes _____   75 calves _____

76 valleys _____   77 sheep _____

78 mice _____   79 batteries _____

80 foxes _____   81 olives _____

Rewrite this passage correctly.

82–94   I can hear something whispered Sandra
so can I confirmed Jess what could it be

_____

_____

_____

_____

Write *did* or *done* correctly in each gap.

95–96   He _____ not do what he should have _____ .

97   She said she had _____ it.

98   Mark _____ his homework yesterday.

Solve the riddles.

In each group of letters there are two words. The letters are in the correct order but the two words are muddled together. Each riddle is an item you might find in a classroom.

99   cpeancsiel   _____

100 codmpuitsekr   _____

Paper 12

This is a passage from a tale of how a little girl named Fern, with the help of a friendly spider, saved her pig Wilbur from the usual fate of nice fat little pigs.

"Charlotte," said Wilbur after a while, "why are you so quiet?"

"I like to sit still," she said. "I've always been rather quiet."

"Yes, but you seem specially so today. Do you feel all right?"

"A little tired, perhaps. But I feel peaceful. Your success in the ring this morning was, to a small degree, my success. Your future is assured. You will live, secure and safe, Wilbur. Nothing can harm you now. These autumn days will shorten and grow cold. The leaves will shake loose from the trees and fall. Christmas will come, then the snows of winter. You will live to enjoy the beauty of the frozen world, for you mean a great deal to Zuckerman and he will not harm you, ever. Winter will pass, the days will lengthen, the ice will melt in the pasture pond. The song sparrow will return and sing, the frogs will awake, the warm wind will blow again. All these sights and sounds and smells will be yours to enjoy, Wilbur – this lovely world, these golden days . . ."

Charlotte stopped. A moment later a tear came to Wilbur's eye. "Oh, Charlotte," he said. "To think that when I first met you I thought you were cruel and bloodthirsty!"

When he recovered from his emotion, he spoke again.

"Why did you do all this for me?" he asked. "I don't deserve it. I've never done anything for you."

"You have been my friend," replied Charlotte. "That in itself is a tremendous thing. I wove my webs for you because I liked you."

From *Charlotte's Web* by E B White

Underline the right answers.

1–2   Who is the discussion in the passage between?
(Fern, Charlotte, Wilbur, Mr Zuckerman)

3   In which season is this passage set?
(summer, spring, autumn, winter)

3

Answer these questions.

4 Why was Wilbur concerned about Charlotte?

_____

5 What happens to the pond as winter turns to spring?

_____

6 Why will the 'warm wind blow again'?

_____

7 What do you think normally happens to 'nice fat little pigs'?

_____

8 Why do you think Wilbur thought Charlotte was 'cruel and bloodthirsty'?

_____

9 Do you think friends are important? Why?

_____

_____

Copy these words adding the missing silent letters, so that each word is spelt correctly.

10 anser _____   11 reck _____

12 casle _____   13 tonge _____

14 lam _____   15 desin _____

16 rubarb _____   17 wite _____

Underline the word which is the same part of speech as the word in bold.

18 **move**   grand   flaky   walk   soft   me

19 **across**   jump   before   river   bridge   wood

20 **your**   her   friend   near   and   boy

21 **because**   reason   safe   hard   and   list

22 **I**   author   person   he   am   boy

23 **crossly**   girl   smart   foe   patiently   friend

24 **cupboard**   pour   hot   drawer   large   the

Write these questions as statements changing as few words as possible

25   Can you see Paul hiding behind the bench?

_____

26   Is the Fish and Chip shop open?

_____

27   Is the homework due in on Monday?

_____

28   Is the tree safe to climb on?

_____

29   Can we go out and play in the snow?

_____

30   Did you bring your coats?

_____

6

Underline the **root words**.

31   agreement   **32**   alphabetical   **33**   impersonal

34   onlooker   **35**   returned   **36**   submerge

37   instruction   **38**   defrosted

8

Write _active_ or _passive_ next to each **sentence**.

39   Bill swam the channel.   _____

40   The sheep were rounded up by the shepherd.   _____

41   Liz kicked the football.   _____

42   The field was flooded with water.   _____

43   Kurt was collected from school by his Dad.   _____

44   Phil caught Tracey's cold.   _____

6

Write a **definition** for each word.

45   lubricate   _____

46   minimum   _____

47 summit _____

48 abbreviate _____

49 obedient _____

50 resolve _____

51 proceed _____

7

Write an **antonym** for the following words by changing the **suffixes**.

52 careful _____   **53** hairless _____

54 painful _____   **55** starry _____

56 useful _____   **57** cloudless _____

6

Rewrite the passage, separating the words correctly and adding the missing capital letters and punctuation.

58–80 asrudijumpedintothepoolalicescreamedshehatedwateronherfacethoughshe
lovedplayingontheinflatablesthatiswhyshehadwantedaswimming
birthdaypartycanyoustopjumpingnearmepleaseaskedaliceaswaterdrippedfrom
hernoseifihavetolaughedrudi

_____

_____

_____

_____

_____

_____

_____

_____

23

With a line, link up the recently coined words with the words they originated from.

81 e-mail   smoke and fog

82 newscast   cheese hamburger

83 heliport   electronic mail

84 cheeseburger   news broadcast

85 smog   helicopter airport

Add a **phrase** or **clause**, to complete each of these sentences.

86 The crowd _____

    were waiting for the football match to begin.

87 Mary wrote a story _____

    which she read out to the class.

Add the missing apostrophes.

88 David wasnt afraid.

89 Gina copied Helens homework.

90–91 Were going to get to Uncle Matts house before it is dark.

92 We could hear the puppies wails.

93 Whats the problem?

94–95 Jacks Mum wouldnt let him play on his bike.

Write an **abbreviation** for each of these.

96 New Zealand   _____

97 Royal Society for the Protection of Birds   _____

98 Save our souls   _____

99 United Arab Emirates   _____

100 Republic of South Africa   _____

First published in 1973 by:
Thomas Nelson and Sons Ltd

This edition in 2001 by:
Nelson Thornes Ltd
Delta Place
27 Bath Road
CHELTENHAM
GL53 7TH
United Kingdom

05 / 10 9 8

A catalogue record for this book is available from the British Library

ISBN 0-7487-6184-5

Illustrations by R Barton and K Kett
Page make-up by Aetos Ltd

Printed in Croatia by Zrinski

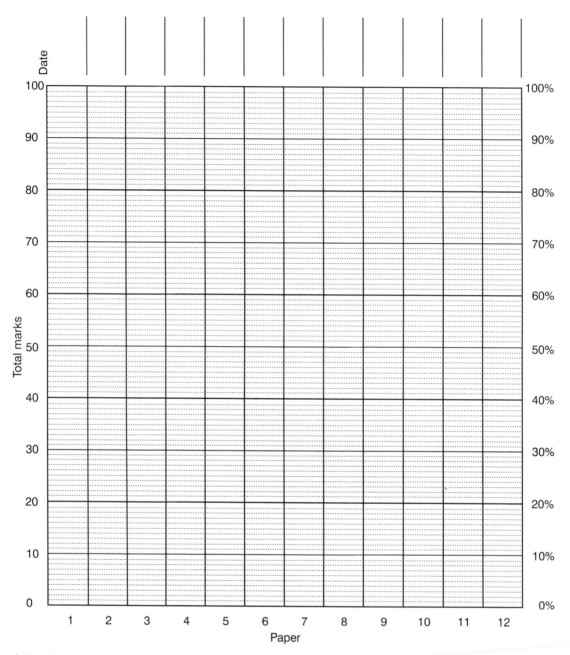

Date

100 — 100%

90 — 90%

80 — 80%

70 — 70%

Total marks

60 — 60%

50 — 50%

40 — 40%

30 — 30%

20 — 20%

10 — 10%

0 — 0%

1 2 3 4 5 6 7 8 9 10 11 12

Paper

Acknowledgements
The authors and publishers wish to thank the following for permission to use copyright material: extract from *A Traveller in Time* by Alison Uttley, reproduced by permission of The Trustees of the Alison Uttley Literary Property Trust; extract from *A Crock of Gold* by Elizabeth Goudge, reproduced by permission of David Higham Associates Ltd; extract from 'Gus the Theatre Cat' from *Old Possum's Book of Practical Cats* by T S Eliot, reproduced by permission of Faber and Faber Ltd; extract from *Charlotte's Web* by E.B. White (Hamish Hamilton 1952) Copyright 1952 J White; extract from *The Hobbit* by J R R Tolkein, reproduced by permission of Harper Collins Publishers Ltd; extract from *Portrait of Pavlo* by Gerald Durrell, reproduced by permission of Curtis Brown Ltd, London, on behalf of Gerald Durrell, Copyright 1973.

Every effort has been made to trace all the copyright holders, but if any have been inadvertently overlooked the publishers will be pleased to make the necessary arrangements at the first opportunity.